Merry Christmas
Sweet heart.
I hope you really
enjoy this book & CD.
Jesus loves you!
Grandma Adelynd
2002

The Greatest Bible Stories Ever Told
Courage & Strength

Stephen Elkins
AUTHOR

Tim O'Connor
ILLUSTRATIONS

BROADMAN & HOLMAN PUBLISHERS
NASHVILLE, TENNESSEE

DAVID AND GOLIATH

1 Samuel 16:7 (For) man looks (on) the outward appearance, but the Lord (God) looks (on) the heart.

Samuel was the last judge to rule Israel. The people of Israel decided they wanted a king, so Samuel chose Saul.

Saul became the first king of Israel.

Israel met the Philistine army on the battlefield. The Israelites made camp on one hill and the Philistines camped on another with a wide valley between them. Now the Philistines had a champion warrior named Goliath. Goliath stood over nine feet tall and carried a heavy javelin and spear. His armor was made of bronze and glistened in the sunlight.

Each morning for forty days the giant Goliath came forward and shouted like thunder, "We don't need to have a war today. Send out one man to fight me. If your man defeats me, all the Philistines will be your slaves. But if I win you will serve us!" King Saul and all the Israelites were terrified. Who could defeat such a giant?

One morning, Jesse, son of Obed, sent his youngest son David to the battlefield to deliver a meal to David's older brothers who were soldiers.

When David arrived and heard Goliath mocking the Lord's army, he said to Saul, "Do not fear this Philistine. I will go and fight him!"

"You? Fight the giant? Why, you're only a boy,"
scoffed Saul. "He is a mighty warrior, a killer. You
are a shepherd boy. You cannot fight him." Then
David answered, "As I kept my father's sheep, I once
fought a lion and rescued the sheep. When the lion
turned on me, I killed it. Later, when a bear came to
take away the sheep, I killed the bear. This giant
will be defeated just like them, for the Lord who
delivered me from the lion and the bear will deliver
me from the hand of this Philistine." Saul said, "Go,
and the Lord be with you!"

David put on Saul's armor, but he was not used to it.
"I cannot wear this armor," David said. So he
gathered his staff, five stones, and his slingshot, and
started walking directly towards Goliath.

When Goliath saw that Israel had sent a young boy
to fight him, he grew angry. "Am I a dog that you
come at me with a stick? Come here and I'll tear you
apart!" Then David spoke, "You come against me
with a sword and a spear, but I come against you in
the name of the Lord Almighty, the God of Israel's
army, whom you mock. This day you will die!"

Goliath was furious and moved in to attack.
But David took out one of the stones
and loaded it into his slingshot.
With all the power of the Lord behind
him, he let it go. Bam! It struck
Goliath right in the forehead
and sank deep.

Goliath staggered, his knees buckled, and he fell like a giant oak tree. Goliath was not dead, so David ran and stood over Goliath. Taking Goliath's own sword, he killed him.

The Lord had given Israel the battle. The Philistine army ran away, but Israel went after them and defeated them. From that day on, David remained in King Saul's service.

Affirmation:
I will stand up
for the Lord!

MIGHTY SAMSON

*Judges 16:28 O Lord (my) God, (please)
remember me ... and strengthen me.*

When Joshua was 110 years old, he died. Joshua's life had
pleased the Lord. But the children and grandchildren of the
Israelites were doing things that did not please the Lord.

On a day when Israel had fallen into sin, the Lord allowed the
Philistines to make them slaves.

At the very same time the angel of the Lord appeared to an Israelite woman who was unable to have children and said, "You will soon have a little baby boy.

Therefore, do not drink any wine while you are pregnant.

When the baby is born, do not cut his hair, for he has been chosen to serve the Lord and deliver Israel from the Philistines."

A little baby boy named Samson was born. He grew to be very strong, and the Lord blessed him.

When Samson became a man, he fell in love with a woman named Delilah. She did not believe in God. The Philistine rulers went to her and said, "Find out what makes Samson so strong and we will give you lots of money." She agreed.

Delilah begged Samson to tell her the secret of his strength, but he would not. Three times she asked, but Samson would not tell her. Finally, he said, "My hair has never been cut, because I was set apart to God since birth. If my head were shaved, I would become as weak as any other man."

So Delilah went straight to the rulers and told them the secret of Samson's strength. That night while Samson slept, she let the Philistines in to shave his head. With his strength gone, Samson was blinded and put into prison. The people celebrated and shouted, "Bring out Samson that he may amuse us!"

They set Samson between the two support pillars of the temple. Now the temple was very crowded that day. Three thousand men and women were on the roof watching.

Then Samson prayed, "O Lord my God, please remember me and strengthen me." Samson gave a mighty push on the pillars. They began to crack into pieces and suddenly, the whole temple fell killing Samson and all the people in it.

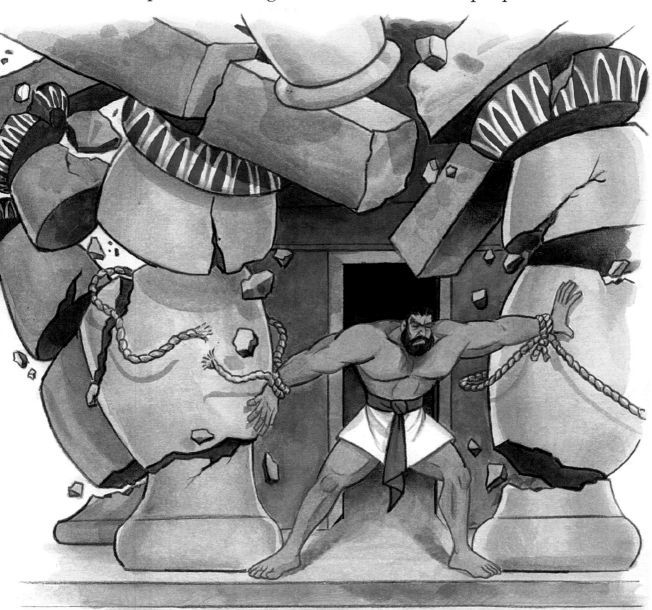

Affirmation: The Lord is my strength!

THE JOURNEY

Exodus 20:2 I am the Lord your God, who brought you out of Egypt.

With the Egyptian army defeated by the Lord, the Israelites began their long journey through the wilderness. They were filled with joy and bound for the promised land. The people feared God and trusted Moses, His servant.

The wilderness was a very harsh and dry place, but the Lord provided sweet water to drink. Each morning the Lord rained down bread from heaven called manna. The people gathered it in baskets, enough for each day. It tasted like wafer cookies made with honey!

After three months of travel, the group reached Mount Sinai where they made camp. Then Moses went up to the mountain where the Lord spoke to him. The Lord said to tell the people of Israel to obey His rules. Then they would be His special people, a holy nation.

Moses returned to the people and told them what God had said. The people agreed to do all the Lord had commanded.

The Lord said He would
come before the people in
a thick cloud. Everyone would hear
Him speak and always trust Moses. He told Moses to have
the people wash and make themselves clean, for in three
days He would come down to Mount Sinai.

On the morning of the third day, there was thunder and
lightning. Then a thick cloud came over the mountain and
a very loud trumpet sounded. Everyone was afraid.

Then Moses led the people to meet with God at the foot of the mountain. It was smoking like a furnace and the whole mountain shook. Moses called out and God answered.

God called Moses to the top of Mount Sinai and spoke these words, "I am the Lord your God who brought you out of Egypt." Then He gave Moses the Ten Commandments.

THE TEN COMMANDMENTS

1. You shall have no other gods but Me.
2. You shall not worship anything you make with your hands that looks like a creation of Mine.
3. You shall not use the name of the Lord to swear or curse.
4. You shall keep the Sabbath Day holy.
5. Honor your father and mother.
6. You shall not commit murder.
7. You shall not commit adultery.
8. You shall not steal.
9. You shall not lie.
10. Do not covet, but be content with what you have.

Affirmation: I will obey the Ten Commandments!

JOB'S TROUBLE

Job 19:25 *I know that my Redeemer lives, and ... in the end he will stand upon the earth.*

Once, in the land of Uz there lived a man named Job. Job and his wife had seven wonderful sons and three beautiful daughters. Job was a good man in the eyes of the Lord and his life was a blessing to others.

Job was also very wealthy. He owned 7,000 sheep, 3,000 camels, 500 oxen, and 500 donkeys, and had many servants. Early in the morning Job would kneel and pray and thank God for his family. He loved them very much.

Now one day in the kingdom of heaven, the angels were coming before the Lord to praise Him. Suddenly, Satan made an appearance. "Where have you come from?" the Lord asked Satan. "I've been roaming the earth, tempting your people to do evil," shouted Satan. "Then you have seen My servant Job," the Lord said. "He hates evil and is always faithful to serve Me." Satan responded, "He only loves You because You protect his family and You've made him very rich. Take that away and he'll hate You!"

"Very well," said the Lord, "I give you permission to test Job. But do no harm to the man."

A few days later a messenger came running to Job and said, "The Sabeans have stolen your oxen and donkeys and killed your servants! I alone have escaped." He had not finished speaking when in came a second servant. "Fire has fallen from out of the sky and burned up all your sheep and your servants! I alone have escaped to tell you." And while he was still speaking, in came a third messenger. "The Chaldeans have attacked us and stolen your camels! They have killed all the servants, and I alone have escaped to tell you."

And before he could finish speaking, in came a fourth servant who said, "Your sons and daughters were together eating dinner when a strong wind suddenly came from the desert and blew down the house, killing them all!"

Job stood before them and sorrow overcame him. His children, his servants, and his possessions were gone! He tore his robe and fell to the ground with a broken heart. He prayed, "I came into this world with nothing. Surely I will leave with nothing. It is the Lord who gives; it is the Lord who has taken away. Praise the name of the Lord!" Job did not blame God for his trouble. This pleased the Lord.

Once again, Satan appeared before the God of Heaven. The Lord spoke, "Your evil schemes have not worked, have they? Job is still faithful to Me!"

Then Satan lashed out, "Yes, but if You allow me to cause him great sickness and pain, he will curse You!"

"Very well," said the Lord, "do as you wish, but do not kill Job." So Satan caused Job's skin to be covered with painful sores from head to toe. Job's heart was breaking for his children, and his body was terribly sick. Job's wife said, "Why should you be faithful to the Lord now? Look at you! Look at our family! You should curse God and die!" But Job replied, "Shall we accept the good and not the trouble?" And again, Job did not blame God.

Job had three close friends who came to comfort him. They hardly recognized their friend because of his sickness and grief. They sat with Job for seven days and nights without saying a word. Finally, Job spoke and cursed the day he was born.

His friend Eliphaz spoke first, "The Lord is correcting you for an evil you have done."

"What kind of friends are you to tell me I have done wrong when I have not?" cried Job.

Then his friend Bildad spoke, "Somewhere, you have forgotten the Lord. So pray that He might forgive you and take away this sickness and pain." Job spoke up, "I have not sinned and all I want to know is why God has done this to me."

Then the Lord spoke to Job out of a storm.

"Now I will ask the questions and you will answer.

Where were you when I created the world, when I gave orders to the morning?

Where were you when I created the seas and formed a man?

Can you speak to the clouds and give strength to all creatures?

Does the hawk fly by your wisdom; does the eagle soar at your command?

Now, do you stand and accuse God Almighty of evil? Answer Me!"

Then Job understood. There are things which we cannot understand, things that only God can know, and we must not question. For men and women are not equal to God. Job bowed his head and prayed, "I am nothing, Lord. Forgive me."

The Lord was pleased with Job and asked him to forgive his friends, for they, too, did not understand the power and greatness of God. After Job had prayed for his friends, the Lord gave Job twice as much as he had before and Job's life was blessed.

Affirmation: I will not blame God for my troubles!

ZACCHAEUS

Luke 19:5 Zacchaeus,
come down immediately.
I must stay at your
house today.

On their way to Jerusalem,
Jesus and His disciples came
to the city of Jericho. It was
the home of a very rich man
named Zacchaeus. He was the chief
tax collector and not liked
by the people.

Zaccheus
wanted to see Jesus,
but he was a very short man and could not see
over the crowds. So he ran ahead and climbed up in
a sycamore tree. From there he could see Jesus as
He passed. When Jesus saw Zaccheus, He said,
"Come down, for I am going to stay at your house today."
At once, Zaccheus jumped down from the tree and welcomed
Jesus into his home.

When the people saw Jesus being kind to Zaccheus, they
were very upset. They didn't know that Zaccheus had
changed! He said to Jesus, "I'm sorry for the way I have
treated the people. I will pay back each one." Jesus was
very happy and replied, "Today you are saved, and that is
why I have come ... to save the lost!"

Affirmation: I want to see Jesus!

THE DAY OF THE LORD

2 Thessalonians 3:3 The Lord is faithful, and He will strengthen and protect you (us).

In Paul's second letter to the Thessalonians he warns the believer that false teachers would come into the church. He writes, "Beware! These teachers will be able to work certain kinds of miracles. But Satan is the source of their power. So pray for us that we may escape their evil traps. For we know the Lord is faithful, and He will strengthen and protect us from the evil one."

Affirmation: The Lord will strengthen and protect me!

THE HUMBLE NEVER CRUMBLE

1 Peter 5:6 Humble yourselves (therefore) under God's mighty hand.

Peter addressed his wonderful letter to God's chosen people. He calls us "strangers in this world." Now strangers are people who have a home somewhere else. They're just visiting for a while. Peter knew that a Christian's true home is in heaven. We live here as "strangers," seeking first the things of God, not the things of gold and glory. This is very strange indeed to worldly people.

But Peter says, "Humble yourselves under God's mighty hand. This means we should set aside our own wants and wishes and do the things that please God. Be self-controlled; for our enemy, Satan, prowls around as a roaring lion, just looking for someone to hurt. Resist him, stand firm in the faith, and he will flee from you. We are truly strangers here, but someday soon we'll be going home to heaven."

Affirmation: I will do things that please God!

COLLECT ALL 10

Word & Song
AUDIO BOOK

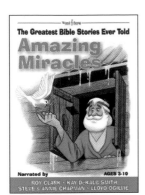
The Greatest Bible Stories Ever Told
Amazing Miracles
Narrated by
ROY CLARK · KAY DeKALB SMITH
STEVE & ANNIE CHAPMAN · LLOYD OGILVIE
AGES 3-10
0-8054-2471-7

The Greatest Bible Stories Ever Told
God's Power
Narrated by
LLOYD OGILVIE · DEAN STONE
GEORGE BEVERLY SHEA
AGES 3-10
0-8054-2466-0

The Greatest Bible Stories Ever Told
Stories of Faith
Narrated by
LARNELLE HARRIS
STEVE & ANNIE CHAPMAN · LLOYD OGILVIE
AGES 3-10
0-8054-2470-9

The Greatest Bible Stories Ever Told
Stories that
Build Character
Narrated by
LARNELLE HARRIS · STEVE GREEN
LLOYD OGILVIE
AGES 3-10
0-8054-2469-5

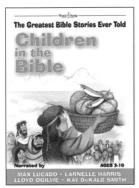
The Greatest Bible Stories Ever Told
Children in the Bible
Narrated by
MAX LUCADO · LARNELLE HARRIS
LLOYD OGILVIE · KAY DeKALB SMITH
0-8054-2474-1

The Greatest Bible Stories Ever Told
Courage & Strength
Narrated by
REGGIE WHITE · LARNELLE HARRIS
STEVE GREEN · LLOYD OGILVIE · STEVE CAMP
AGES 3-10
0-8054-2468-7

The Greatest Bible Stories Ever Told
Friendship & Kindness
Narrated by
MAX LUCADO · REBECCA ST JAMES
LARNELLE HARRIS · TWILA PARIS · STEVE GREEN
AGES 3-10
0-8054-2473-3

The Greatest Bible Stories Ever Told
The Good Shepherd
Narrated by
STEVE GREEN
JERRY FALWELL · ANNIE CHAPMAN
AGES 3-10
0-8054-2475-X

The Greatest Bible Stories Ever Told
Prayer & Promise
Narrated by
MAX LUCADO · GEORGE BEVERLY SHEA
STEVE GREEN · ADRIAN ROGERS · LLOYD OGILVIE
AGES 3-10
0-8054-2472-5

The Greatest Bible Stories Ever Told
Special Families
JONI EARECKSON TADA · TWILA PARIS · STEVE GREEN
LLOYD OGILVIE · STEVE & ANNIE CHAPMAN
0-8054-2467-9

Available in Your Favorite Christian Bookstore.

We hope you enjoyed this Word & Song Storybook.